Happiness in Your Life ⸴ Book Three: Forgiveness

Doe Zantamata

DEDICATION

For us.

CONTENTS

ACKNOWLEDGMENTS

Thank you to all those who have been with me on
this journey, even if just for a little while.
Thank you to you who is reading this book for our
connection within these pages and beyond.

1 WHAT FORGIVENESS IS AND IS NOT

Most people think forgiveness means to erase an event from memory and go on with life as it was before. That's not forgiveness, that's willful denial, and can be the cause of getting stuck in some awful places.

Why do so many people not know what forgiveness is and think that it's something that it totally is not, never was, and could be harmful if attempted?

The answer is surprisingly obvious but it happened so long ago you probably didn't give it a re-evaluation.

Does this sound vaguely familiar from your childhood?

You: He hit me

Him: I did not!

Parent (to him): Say you're sorry!

Him (reluctantly and without meaning): Sorry

Parent (to you): Now say you forgive him

You (reluctantly and with a heavy feeling in your chest): I forgive you

Parent: Ok now go play.

Your parent was doing what they learned. Your parent was doing what they thought was right. Your parent was attempting to finish talking on the phone or watching their show and just wanted you kids to get along and play nicely. So this little script was introduced and it didn't feel right or genuine at the time, nor the many thousands of times it was repeated in the home, at friends houses, in school, at camp, and every time a conflict arose in your childhood.

What it taught you was that "forgiveness" meant someone with no remorse saying *sorry* was a pass key to you having to pretend like the offense never even happened and resume life as it was before.

With two little kids playing, not a huge obvious problem.

But in life, if you believe this is what forgiveness is, it can be a horrible, decades long struggle in many ways.

Let's get clear on what forgiveness is.

1. Forgiveness is about the past and only about the past.

2. Forgiveness is letting go of resentment towards a person or event. To forgive is just to accept that what happened has happened and cannot be changed, ever. It's past, it's gone. And to stop giving your attention, anger, and power to it (once you have processed and healed).

That's it.

That is *it*.

Now equally as important, let's look at what forgiveness **isn't**.

1. Forgiveness does not depend on the involvement of another person. Forgiving someone is between you and your mind and heart and doesn't need to involve another person or people at all.

2. Forgiveness doesn't guarantee a person a spot in your present or future. It's not a free pass for them to avoid punishment or repercussions or to carry on the way they did before. If a person is still to be in your life present and future, that has nothing to do with forgiving them. You can forgive someone and still think they are a jerk. You can forgive someone and not talk to them as much or have them as close in your life as they were before. You can forgive someone and sue them for damages. You can forgive someone fully without them ever even knowing you have, and never speak to or see them again.

Forgiveness takes place in your heart and frees you from a prison of pain.

What determines if you'll see or speak to them again is **trust**, not forgiveness.

Can you trust that they won't repeat the same action or actions that caused you pain?

There are plenty of times when you **can** trust that a person won't repeat the action...

> ➤ if it happened by accident

> ➤ if it really was a miscommunication

> ➤ if they show true remorse not just a weak apology

> ➤ if they make amends

> ➤ if they promise to be transparent

> ➤ if they take responsibility for their action or actions

...many things would provide the trust to continue the relationship. Maybe not the exact same as before, depending on the situation.

But,

If this is something...

> that happened more than once

> that happens all the time

> if they were not forthcoming and were caught instead of confessed

> if they dismiss, diminish, or try to justify what they did

> if they blame someone else, or if they try to turn it around and blame you

> if they do it on purpose

> if they don't seem to understand what they did that hurt you even when you try to communicate it with them

...you can't trust that they won't do it again.

In fact, they likely will.

At that point, you have to create boundaries,

7

distance, or even end the relationship altogether. Even if you love them. Even if you want to give them "just one more" chance to redeem themselves, and even if you really thought you had a future with them.

You'll just be setting yourself up for more pain and when it happens again you'll have to not only forgive them but also yourself for knowing better and allowing yourself to get hurt anyway.

Now, you may have guilt thrown on you but let's make one thing perfectly clear. It's not "you being unforgiving" to let them go, it's "them being untrustworthy" and you deciding to protect yourself in the present and future.

Of course if it's an ex-spouse and you have underage children to co-parent, you can't just never speak to them again. That wouldn't be legal, nor good for the children. If they're really horrible, arrange to meet only with a co-parenting counselor and really limit the amount you interact with them to only what is necessary. Sometimes people will be angry at you just for leaving even though they are the ones who caused you to leave. They will try to seek revenge and cause you pain because they think it will make them feel superior or that they have power over you. You can't change that about them if they've chosen to do it either consciously or subconsciously but you can control how you react and respond to what they are doing. Keep your power. Don't let them steal more of your peace from you.

2 FORGIVING YOUR PARENTS

You may be wondering why we're starting with "forgiving your parents" before "forgiving yourself." Well, under the age of 7 years old, we're basically sponges. We learn who we are, how the world is, how people interact, what love is and isn't....from our parents. Other adult role models, too, but mostly our parents. So we start with forgiving them, otherwise when we look at forgiving ourselves for things, it would be too easy to deflect blame on what we learned from them was "normal."

Forgive Your Parents : Legacy Pain and "Original Sin"

Original Sin is of course the Adam and Eve story in Christianity in the Garden of Eden. Using this concept, whether you are Christian or not, you can see how the wisdom of it applies to each person's life on Earth.

1. Original Sin in the Bible is the eating of the apple from the Tree of Knowledge when told not to by God and getting kicked out of Eden.

So what if this represents family trauma? There is trauma in every family line that is passed down, flipped around, on to each next generation like a hot coal that never cools down or gets extinguished. It burns each person who touches it in a different way, and each blames the one who passed it down to them for the wounds. Babies are born pretty blissful and until the parents start raising them and putting their ways of the world onto them, none of the legacy pain is passed down to them.

2. The way out of original sin is rebirth through baptism/christening and taking Christ into one's heart.

Rebirth is done by accepting all that is "Christ" or God-like into one's heart, and a leaving behind of all that's happened to that point in life. The ultimate themes of God and Heaven are forgiveness and love. So here's the amazing part. When you realize that the pain you endured as a child by your parents had nothing to do with you, and that it was unknowingly passed down by them from their parents who received them from their parents and so on...you can see how no one and everyone are at fault all at once. Once you're grown, you can't go back to childhood and erase it all and start again. But anger is dissolved by compassion, so having the realization that they as small children were covered in false beliefs that caused them pain can dissolve your anger. Forgiveness, remember is just acceptance that a circumstance or event happened and cannot be changed and then leave it there. These are hardest to do with family trauma because they are the first, closest, most dependent, and most important relationships at least of our early lives. They shape who we are for life. So to forgive doesn't mean you all of a sudden understand that they were hurt and they didn't understand what they were doing to you so it's fine. Not at all. It's saying you understand that any pain or abuse that was put on you by them had nothing to do with you and you can understand, not excuse but understand, that it also was passed down to them. You can then say the legacy of pain in your family line stops here. Right here, right now. Set down that burning hot coal at your feet and extinguish the heat, flame, and burning ability that it has. No more hell. No more passing it on down to future generations.

Forgive your parents : the Experiences that never happened

We'll go to Disney! We'll move into a house! We'll go next summer, next year…and then it was over. For some parents, they actually meant to get or do those things but they weren't financially able. Some procrastinated. Some actually didn't even mean it they just said it to make you be quiet and leave them alone. Whatever the reason, it all needs to be forgiven. If it's not, you'll over react whenever someone tries to put you off, even for little things. The unhealed wounds hurt even when someone barely touches them. Heal them to be able to discern small, medium sized, and enormous situations today instead of having even a hint of the painful past ones feel like the world is coming to an end. And the belief that you'll be let down, disappointed, or cast aside will be recreated in your life by those you choose and how you react until it's forgiven and the belief is changed.

Write down the promises that were made but never kept. Read them over even though it will probably cause you to feel sad, disappointed, uncomfortable, even angry. So look at them and acknowledge that it sucks and that those things won't ever happen for your child self. Accept that it's too late for your child self.

Your child self had some beliefs shaped in him or her that they were powerless and unimportant. To focus forward, change the beliefs and take time to affirm or meditate on how good and empowering the new beliefs feel. The old beliefs felt powerless, unchangeable or stuck, and so disappointing. So now the new beliefs; that you are in control of your life, and that you choose good people to be with and have fun, positive experiences that become beautiful memories. Maybe it doesn't seem true right from the start, but maybe you'll remember a few good times with good people when you start to really affirm these beliefs. There is proof in our history of a lot of different stories. The ones we believe the most are the ones we will focus on and will stand out to tell the tale that supports them. As you keep affirming them, you'll be able to consciously recognize in your daily life when they are confronted. You won't just fall back into the old program and the old resentments but in present day. You'll be able to voice as an adult when you disagree, what you'd like, and what you don't like without subconsciously fearing that you can't speak up because it will get you in trouble or won't change anything anyway.

Forgiving Your Parents: What You Didn't Get Means You Got Something Else, Instead

When you look to your past, you may feel grateful or broken-hearted, depending on what you believe you were given or deprived of in those early years.

Realize though, that for everything that you were given, you were deprived of something else, and for everything you were deprived of, you received something else instead.

If you received encouragement, you were deprived of discovering self-worth independent of external validation of others. Those who grew up in a non-encouraging environment are perceived to be utterly fearless. But the truth is, they were given an early opportunity to develop validation from within without the requirement of external support.

Those who were given encouragement must develop independent self-worth in adulthood. They are prone to bending over backwards in an attempt to try to please an unpleasable boss or spouse, as the concept of disapproval is so very foreign to them.

So is it better to give a child no encouragement? Of course not. But if you happen to be an adult in despair over not receiving any, recognize your gift, and use it well. You can't change the past, so you may as well take everything positive that it gave you and apply those gifts ~ no matter how painful they once were ~ to your present and future happiness.

If a child was made to continue with an athletic or music program, they can say they learned commitment or they may believe that they were forced to do what they didn't want to do. If a child was allowed to quit said programs they could say they were allowed to decide for themselves or they could say they wish their parent had made them continue because of how good they'd be at it now. It really is what you decide to take from it.

If you moved around a lot you may feel like you don't have any roots, but if you didn't move at all you may feel like you're afraid of change and get stuck easily. But the positive sides of each of those is that the first child was given the knowledge to know you can move when you don't like where you are, and the second child can know that it's possible to stay where you are and make things work when they change. And both as adults can develop a discernment for when it's time to move versus when it's better to stay.

You've got to take what you got and recognize and appreciate it, and give yourself what you didn't get.

That's the only way to make them all worthwhile.

What a lot of people do who are unaware and had

an extreme type of parent is decide consciously or unconsciously to be the opposite to their child. Well the opposite of unhappy is still unhappy, just in a different way. That pendulum swing can then go back and forth down generations as a legacy.

For example if a parent was overbearing or controlling, maybe even with good intentions, say to keep the child safe, that child may grow up to feel very insecure and resentful of the parent for not allowing them to make decisions and to grow. So to their own child they may decide they will be the exact opposite. Their intentions are also good, but that child may end up feeling resentful that their parent didn't seem to care, didn't teach them things, didn't guide them. So what happens? They decide to be the exact opposite to their child and the cycle continues. This can also happen with addiction where the child of an alcoholic may completely abstain and then have a zero tolerance of alcohol for their own child who then rebels after feeling restricted and gets into trouble with alcohol.

How does forgiveness play into this? Well, when you haven't forgiven, you're going to be hyper-sensitive to that which caused your pain. Like an open wound, if anyone gets near it, it hurts. The wound has to be healed before you can have actual discernment and be able to practice balance or moderation instead of extremes.

Adults who haven't forgiven their parents for traumatic experiences can also remain in a childlike state emotionally and not realize that as they grew into adults, they have the power they didn't have as children. So instead of acting in empowerment, they resort to childish tactics like lying or manipulation in order to try to get what they think they want. Emotional immaturity is often called "narcissism" and from the outside the two can look very similar. But what you're getting with an emotionally immature person is an alternating of an emotional aged 5 year old in an adult body who adores you and wants to do everything to please you versus their inner emotional 14 year old who rebels against you. You're never actually dealing with an adult. That 5 year old is sweet and endearing and feels safe to love and one who is so vulnerable that you can't help but want to care for him or her. But then the rebellious 14 year old shows up and you don't even recognize this person who now lashes out at you and is so filled with anger that you are more in a state of shock than anything else. Where's it coming from?? It's not coming from you, it's coming from ages old pain that's never been addressed and released and a recreated pattern that has triggered it all over again. But until they realize they are the ones who are creating this, it will seem like reality to them and you will alternate between soul mate and mortal enemy. The only thing stable about it is the instability it's guaranteed to bring.

If you don't forgive your parents, your subconscious will recreate and repeat those battles throughout your life. If you heard yourself in times of least empowerment and highest frustration, you may be repeating things you thought or said to one of your parents as a child. Work and career tend to be more father based, and romantic or very close friendships tend to be more mother based. You may choose people or be attracted to people and situations who will fulfill those roles. The child forever seeks to win the fight. But winning the fight means maturing through, forgiving the past, and accepting that it was how it was and can't be changed. Winning means to discover who you are as an adult, what you want out of life, work, romantic, and friend relationships, and move towards and create those.

You may never have learned how to decide what you actually want or what's right for you. If you were in an abusive or even overly strict childhood, you may have learned to keep your thoughts to yourself and become aware of what you think the parent wants so that you can avoid being in trouble or being hurt. That may have helped you survive childhood, but it will destroy all of your adult relationships. Recreating that method will have you assume the role of positive and agreeable partner at first, followed by resentful that you never get what you want or it's all about them. This may seem very real to you but the truth was, you built that via dishonesty from day one. You'll only change what you see as a problem, so if you label your actions as "easy going" or think your motives are "if you're happy, I'm happy," you won't change them. It's only if you call them dishonest and realize the fear underneath was that if you actually said what you wanted or didn't want, you'd be rejected…that's when you can see how flawed your methods were and the need to change them.

It doesn't even have to be an abusive childhood in the physical sense. It could be a helicopter mom who was trying to give you everything she never had but let you know in no uncertain terms how lucky you were and how good you had it compared to her childhood. Your fear of disappointing her could cause you to assume that same role because you had the weight of not only her approval of you but the job of trying to heal her pain from her childhood and that was just too tall an order for any human being, especially a little one.

So regardless of your childhood, you have to ask yourself now, "Do I feel like I get what I want in life? Or for some reason do I feel that in order for others to be happy I must bury my needs and sacrifice, that there isn't a possibility of everyone being happy?"

If you hide your wants and needs, you erase even the possibility for compromise or finding solutions that work for everyone.

If you answered, "yes," to those questions, the first thing to do is get out a fresh journal or even a sheet of paper and make some lists. Get to know you. If you've never even considered your wants and needs, this will be an introduction of sorts and it may surprise you. Maybe your wants and needs really aren't that huge or unrealistic at all, and learning how to voice them and receive them with gratitude can totally change formerly unfulfilling dynamics that have been at play your whole life.

Make a list of

1. What you want out of a friendship.

2. What you want out of a romantic relationship (if you want one).

3. What you want out of work, whether it be a job or your own business.

4. What you want out of any other type of relationship; maybe even that of the ones with your adult children or relatives

You don't have to do this all in one day. In fact, it probably wouldn't be a very good set of lists if you did. We're digging through some very old brain filing cabinets here. You can even start with one or two things and think about it or have it buzzing around your mind a few days and add some more.

Now don't automatically think this is a selfish, jerk set of lists to make. That may be your initial reaction and that will be as a result of past conditioning that made you feel guilty for actually having *any* wants or needs.

Yes, being selfless is good. But being self-absolutely-nothing is not good. It's not good for anyone else or for you. It will only end up making you feel burnt out, unappreciated, used, and resentful. Healthy relationship dynamics have a flow back and forth of giving and receiving. If the flow is only one way, well of course that will end with one being all used up and the other then seeking someone else to receive from and/or someone who doesn't reject receiving back.

What these lists will show you are places where you've been neglecting yourself and choosing others who will assist in the neglect. Once you shift within and put these things into practice, your outer world will change. Not all right away like a magic trick because realizing is different than changing habits. Realizations can happen in an instant but habits can take days, weeks, or even years to change.

What you'll notice over time though is that some people will split because you'll no longer be who they were seeking. If they actually did want someone to use and didn't want to give anything back, they will not find that in you anymore and will eventually go seek it in someone else. Some will adapt and you'll discover that you actually like them a lot more now. You'll learn that it's really nice to be considered, to receive care, and to be valued. It makes you respect and think more highly of those people in your life, and it gives you greater confidence in how much they care about and value you – you as a person – not you as a doer of things for them. There will likely be guilt at first, associated with not being a constant outflow but you can dissolve the guilt by realizing that people who do value you, do consider you, and do want to give and care to and for you are people who want to do so.

Side-note and this isn't scientifically proven so don't take it as Gospel, but there are some theories that illnesses can manifest in people who are constant outflow-only givers and over-carers. Chronic pain and other illnesses that force the person to stop and receive because they physically have to. Louise Hay's work delves much deeper into that in "You Can Heal Your Life," and the jury is out on exactly how certain that all is, but there is something to think about there, even with regards to karma.

Let's say you've been caring for your spouse and family to a fault and have been unaware and refused any care at all but have felt taken for granted or overworked and burnt out. If a chronic illness manifested and you literally had to say no to even the simplest things, that would force your spouse to take on a greater role and to care for you. If that spouse took on the role and was dedicated to your care, that would be a return of the one-sided care you had been putting out for many years before.

Again, do not take this to mean that oh everyone who develops MS, fibromyalgia, or even cancer has brought it on themselves by overdoing care for everyone else and never receiving because that makes it seem like an unfair punishment for a person being "too good" and that wouldn't seem right or good at all. If life really is only about love and learning, and a flow of giving and receiving, it would fit within all of those parameters. And there would still be choices to make when given those circumstances; the person who usually cared for everyone may become miserable and feel useless when they're unable to continue to be in the only role they've ever known instead of receiving care with gratitude. Or the person who had been cared for may choose to abandon the person who became ill and seek out someone else who will over care for them and is physically able to do so. So along those lines, it's not about fairness but it is about choices and consequences.

3 FORGIVE YOURSELF

If you ever talk about yourself in the past and hear yourself saying mean things like, "I was so stupid," or "I was such a jerk," or "I was so ignorant," that needs to stop, pronto. It means that you haven't forgiven your younger self and that younger self is still a part of you today.

Probably most of the mean things you did or said were out of insecurity or fear. Well, when you're young, unless you're superhuman, insecurity and fear are a part of life. It's a big world with a lot of people in it and that is intimidating! The later childhood and early teen years have folks beginning to see differences in each other and compare. They see societal ideals in magazines, online, on TV, and in movies and feel like they fall short in so many areas. This increases the insecurity and fosters the dynamic of inferior and superior. Kindergarten age children don't bully each other. They haven't learned this foolish lesson of society yet. They haven't been made to feel ugly or like a loser or that they don't fit in. Once those things enter their, and at one time your psyche, they fester and develop. So to be mad at yourself for at one time possessing them isn't fair to you. Under the age of seven we're all just sponges, learning how the world works. We're driven by instinct, avoid danger or things that scare you in order to survive. So some children learn and absorb that empathy and compassion and that it's not right to do or say things to people that are hurtful. But some don't learn those things and aren't even conscious of them. Some people who are 75 years old don't seem to have ever learned those things! When you learn them, whatever age you are, when you absorb them, it can cause you to look back with regret and shame on your past behavior. You've got to forgive yourself for not knowing what you didn't know before you learned it. Denial won't help, won't fool anyone for very long, and will only cause you to be mean to anyone who comes near the door of your house of truth. To keep shaming yourself for the rest of your life isn't fair or helpful either. If you were to cause a car accident and hurt someone you'd make amends, learn to be more careful, and move on with your life. Before you truly absorb and know empathy, it's all an accident. Even what you thought at the time was on purpose. Having power over someone by making them feel small or unworthy never made you larger or worthier...after the ego surge, your conscience told you that you weren't acting like a good person for it and it was right. Trying to prove superiority only proves insecurity. But that can take awhile to learn. But once you learn it, you've got to forgive yourself not just for you, but for everyone else you encounter in life.

Here's why:

By continuing to punish and berate yourself, who is it helping?

Besides keeping your guilty conscience alive, it doesn't help *anyone*.

As long as you hold beliefs that you are unworthy and should be ashamed of yourself for life, you're going to be limited in your own abilities and how much joy you believe you deserve to receive. Insecurity causes mean behavior towards others and self-shaming causes insecurity. If you want to be able to be kind to others, you've got to release yourself from the shame prison you've put yourself in. There's no other way out...you hold both the lock and the key. If you practice the Law of Attraction, you may have great things, great opportunities, and great people show up in your life and then just as quickly leave. Self-sabotage and not feeling worthy or deserving of those great things and people in life is one of the surest ways to make sure that you'll see them and have high hopes, then be anywhere from disappointed to crushed when they disappear. Even if you don't practice the Law of Attraction, subconsciously not believing you're worthy of good people will cause you to act out without realizing it. You'll push them away with snide remarks, questioning why they're around you, or putting yourself down (even in humor) which will increase the longer and closer they are to you. You may not even notice you're doing it because it's coming from that subconscious self of yours that believes you really don't deserve them. This eventually will hurt you when they leave, but up until that point, it's hurting them and they'll have no idea why you're doing it. They don't know the things you may be trying to hide out of shame. You could be a much better friend or partner to them if you'd truly forgive yourself and be present with them free of that inner burden.

If you don't forgive yourself, you'll also be less forgiving to others who act in ways that remind you of your younger self. If you hold yourself to being an idiot then, you'll hold them to being an idiot now. When they are about to go through, to learn a similar life lesson that you learned, if you have not realized that some lessons need to be lived through to be learned and forgiven yourself for not knowing what you couldn't possibly have known, you may inadvertently direct all that anger and resentment towards them. You may feel intense passion in trying to warn them not to do what you did and even more intense emotion when they do it anyway.

You'll get very angry with them and won't accept that they haven't reached a point yet where they see things as you do now. You may try to teach them or punish them but the truth is that they'll only see things when they're ready to and from their experience, not your words. Unless it's a literal life or death situation, you've got to step back and let them learn their way through in their own time. If you try to become their conscience, in a non life or death scenario, especially in matters of the heart, you won't be helping. You'll be adding pressure and if you add too much, they may rebel and go stronger and faster towards what you're trying to warn them about as a reaction against feeling controlled by you. Nobody wants to feel stupid. Or controlled. Or belittled...and even if your most honest intention is to try to prevent them from enduring pain that you endured, before they've lived it, it won't be received that way at all.

Back to you. Forgive yourself for not knowing what you didn't know before you learned it. Find gratitude and compassion for that young woman or young man who was struggling along and making some bad choices, unaware of the consequences that would follow. It was all part of the learning process. Remember for life that people act in ways they later regret when they're operating out of insecurity or fear or both. You can't change the past, you can only learn from it and do better today.

Release the false belief that thinking more would have saved you. You were not stupid for not knowing what you didn't know. Even if other people tried to warn you. Even if you had a feeling every now and again but did it anyway. Hold yourself accountable only for what you know today. You can't hold yourself accountable for what you didn't, and couldn't possibly have known. It's just not fair. If I ask you to describe a place you've never been, how well would you do? What if other people describe it to you first? Unless and until you actually go there and live it, it's impossible. But once you live it, you know what it's like and can describe it in detail. And you can know to go somewhere similar or to avoid places like it based on that knowing that's only come from living it. Life is love, learning, and experiencing. Not just "the good parts." It's all of it. To regret any part of your past means to regret learning, which means to regret one of the main points of life! Appreciate it all for what it gave you, taught you, shaped you, and appreciate yourself for making it through the struggle.

You were who you were then but release any bad feelings and you'll free yourself from punishment and free others from judgment. You are who you are now, wiser and better for your experiences, both the good ones and the bad.

Forgive Yourself – Romantic Relationships

If you really take responsibility for all your actions, you'll realize that after a bad break up, you're not really mad at them.

You're mad at yourself for putting up with their nonsense after they showed you they were full of nonsense.

You're mad at yourself for failing to make them into a better person.

You're mad at yourself for not accepting that you can't change a person, even if you truly believe that them changing would have been better for both of you.

You saw them lie to other people but you still didn't think they were lying to you.

You denied your eyes and got hurt with what you already knew. It's their right to choose how to behave (even if it's like a jerk) and it's not your decision for them to stop behaving like a jerk, it's theirs. It's only your decision to be with someone who chooses to behave like a jerk or not.

Forgive yourself.

You tried to do what you thought was right but you were trying to do the impossible. A person can only change themselves. It's not your job or your right to try to make them be any different than they are.

4 FORGIVING EXES AND THOSE WHO ARE OUT OF YOUR LIFE

Forgiving those who are out of your life.

Some people don't realize the value of forgiving those who are out of their lives, but it really is for you. For your peace of mind and ability to move on in your life.

Imagine you owned a store with beautiful ceramic pots. One day a man came into your store, looked right at you, then angrily shoved one of the pots off a shelf right by the front door and it crashed onto the floor. He then ran out, or you told him to get out, and you never saw him again.

Now you still have work to do, even though you did nothing wrong and didn't deserve it.

See, what most people do outside of this story – in real life – is blame that person forever and never clean up the mess. But you can see it more clearly in this story...that you *do* actually have a choice of what to do and what your choices will lead to. If in this story you left it there, every new person who walked through the door would see the mess of broken pottery and ask what happened and you'd tell them about this awful man and what he did and you relive and repeat the energy daily and it would become a solid victim story. Everyone would empathize and agree with you he should not have done it and he should come back and clean it up and pay for a new one. But we all know that would never happen.

So forgiveness is again letting go of resentment towards a person or event...accepting that it happened and cannot be changed, and moving on.

So what you would do is clean up the broken

pieces and throw them out. You would buy anot..
pot and place it on the shelf...if not the exact same
one then one equally as beautiful or even better.
People walking into your shop would say hello and
look at all the beautiful pots and never know about
the awful man or what he did. You would be able to
enjoy your time with them without reliving what he
did and using up your precious and valuable time
with them telling them the sordid tale of the pot
smasher.

Now apply that to real life...if not a man or a pot
that was broken, imagine it was a person or people
and what they broke was trust, agreements, your
heart...it may not seem like you have a choice to
sweep up the pieces broken on the floor, but you do.
And fact is, it's more difficult if you've already
gotten in the habit of leaving them there and telling
every new person who comes into your life about
your old war stories and feeling that they care and
empathize. Maybe you feel that if they know what
you've been through they will empathize with you
and they would treat you better. But honestly,

would treat you poorly would do so ɏ heard what happened. People who you well will treat you well even if they've *never* heard what happened. Maybe you believe this story is part of you and by not telling people, you're hiding a part of yourself but it's not. Don't be attached to the pain of your life. Find the lesson and live with that. The lesson of valuing honest, good people and valuing trust. The realization that not every person is a good person and so when you do find someone who is you enjoy your time together with them and show them how much you appreciate them. Those are the things to carry with you, not the pain.

Forgiveness is For You, Not For Them

You've no doubt heard this statement before but have you realized why it is so true? Resentment is a burden you carry that you wake up and remind yourself of and take into another day. You take it into another job, another relationship, or another experience. It clouds the optimism that should be there. It robs you of the hope and faith you had before the experience happened. The resentment, not the event, wrecks your life.

When you choose to set down that resentment, accept that it happened and can't be changed, you take your life back. You take your optimism, hope, and faith back. You enter into each new day free of that anger, sadness, and regret.

You get to live again, resilient.

There's another saying, "it can make you bitter or better." Same thing. You can emerge from the experience bitter for the rest of your life, or wiser for the experience not to repeat it, but untarnished by the pain of it. Getting knocked down was not your choice but getting back up and moving forward is totally up to you.

No one holds that power over your happiness unless you live on repeat and continue to give your power away to a shadow of the past.

Forgiving a *Very* Damaging Relationship

It could be a marriage, a boyfriend or girlfriend, or even a very close friend. Some relationships are so damaging that when it's all done you feel you're burnt out and had the life sucked out of you. Worse yet, the "ex" will often move on quickly and you still feel stuck and in a rut and unable to stop the awful memories on repeat.

In simple terms, when you're the user, you move on to a new person to use. You've invested nothing and taken everything. When you're the used, you're left as a shell of who you once were, having invested everything you had into someone who really wasn't worth it at all. It's normal to feel as though you've lost yourself and been through a war.

It's normal to have flashbacks of memories and see them differently and with anger. Your self worth was eroded and your focus was on the impossible and fruitless pursuit of trying to make them happy. You forgot you. You extended yourself thinking it would be appreciated but instead that became the new standard of what you were expected to do. What a mess. What an awful *wish you could go back in time and walk the other way* mess.

But here's the thing: You can't.

The only way to get through this is to heal from it and build a new life for yourself.

If you were hit by a bus, you know as soon as that bus pulled away you wouldn't be healed, right? But with an emergency room visit, some casts, rest, physical therapy, and time, you would heal. Maybe not fully but with a lot of luck and determination you'd be better and better than the day you were hit.

So in a relationship like this, you were mentally and emotionally hit by a bus. And not just once, but many times. Your healing won't be instant the moment it finally ends, but with time, therapy of many types, and determination, you will heal. Therapy can be traditional therapy, self-help books, religious guidance, trips to the beach, meditation, surrounded by the company of good friends...or all of the above.

You've got to start building a new life that's completely yours and that is good, great, and then amazing. That's a tall and overwhelming order for someone who has just been hit by a bus and has zero energy or motivation to just hop up and start living the ideal stock photo life. But you don't have to do it all today. You don't have to do it all next week, next month, or even next year. You have to rest and decompress and go through the grief of it in your own time. Maybe you're just plain feral for a month or two and feeling and releasing that anger through fully embracing the victim part of it via journaling and the patient ear of a friend who has been there or a therapist who has seen it before are what you need at this point to heal. The anger is actually a great sign. If your self worth were still as low as it was at the lowest, you wouldn't feel anger. The anger comes when your self worth begins to bounce back and you revisit those memories from a higher self love level. What can also come in here though is anger at yourself for believing, for putting up with, for sticking around when there couldn't possibly be any more reasons to have left and the whole thing was a big, red flag. So forgive yourself. Forgive yourself for not knowing what you didn't know before you learned it. We get fed all kinds of crazy stuff like *real love means you stick through the bad times* and *to be good you must be loyal* and that you should love someone through the turbulence. Well ok If someone has an illness or something out of their control and you don't abandon them, that's one thing. But if someone is just a willful jerk and will take as much as you give and ask for more, that's not building a relationship, it's just destroying you. It's not proving your love, it's proving how much garbage you'll put up with. But often it was a gradual thing and it was hard to discern at the time when you should have opted out or it was a roller coaster of good and bad and you thought ignoring the bad would make it go away and eventually the good would win out. You thought they'd see how much you love them but instead they just learned how little respect you would tolerate. Whatever the case, you've got to forgive yourself. You weren't stupid. You thought you were doing the loving thing, the kind thing, the patient thing. You didn't realize you were abandoning yourself. Come back to you now.

If ever in your life you've needed your own love, it's now.

And remember, you can forgive someone and still think they are a jerk. Or maybe you have more information on their upbringing or things that happened in their life and so you have a little more compassion and see them as damaged or broken in some ways and that acting like a jerk is their survival mechanism because to them, vulnerability is a terrifying thing that means they will be attacked, hurt, or destroyed. So they put up a wall, push people away, treat people horribly so that they will leave....and aren't even aware of what they are doing to others and to themselves.

Even if you pointed it out.

Even if you were a safe and loving person.

Even if you didn't deserve any of the lies, betrayal, or hurt they caused you.

Even if they claimed to love you.

Forgiving them means you set all that down and learn, I mean REALLY learn that you can't fix a person with love and patience and putting up with being hurt. They have to want to fix themselves for themselves and not just to keep you. Otherwise they'll just resent you for wanting to "change them."

It can't come from the outside.

It has to come from within.

But...louder and for those in the back, forgive yourself.

5 FORGIVENESS: THE PROCESS

The process of forgiveness basically has four steps:

1. Acceptance

2. Reflection

3. Wisdom

4. Presence

Remember, forgiveness is for you.

Belief drives reality, not the other way around. You can't have it both ways, either you carry the belief that they ruined your life or the belief that

a negative impact on it for awhile, but you
.ing and your life is becoming amazing. See if
y~~ ~ with the first belief, you will continue to
bring it into the present. Say it was an ex
relationship that was so awful; betrayal, lies,
mistreatment of all types...an emotional buffet of
horrible. So if you don't forgive that, the absolute
best person in the world could show up and that
new relationship would be quickly poisoned by the
past one. You would push them away with
passionate stories about how awful the other person
was, mistrust towards them because you don't want
to make that mistake again and think they need to
earn your trust....well no one who is a good person
wants that. They want to get to know someone,
share good times with them, share experiences and
learn about new things. If you're still living in the
past, there's no room for that to happen. If you go to
a dinner date and instead of enjoying the dinner
drudge up an unforgiven memory of when that ex
got drunk and argued with you on Valentine's Day
three years ago, well that's just soiled up this date
and the memory of this date forever. Imagine that

you have a choice between an old photo album of pictures you can't stand or a brand new camera. Which will you bring with you everywhere you go in life? Which will you focus on and live in? It is up to you. You are not powerless over where you allow your thoughts to go and repeat.

Forgiveness allows you a clean slate and fresh start to life at any point. It removes the shackles of the pain of the past and frees you up to become your truest self, to feel joy, to achieve, to love...fully.

So *why do people* hold on to that old, awful stuff?

Well, often it's because they just haven't realized they don't have to. Literally that simple. Like the old hot coal analogy, they're standing there screaming about how much it hurts to hold that hot coal but yet they still stand there holding it. Set it down. Detach. Heal. Move forward with your life. It only makes sense to do that...to not hurt any longer than you have to.

As life goes on, pretty much everyone will have had their heart broken, been hurt, betrayed, deceived, manipulated…all sorts of rotten stuff. It's not *all* of life and it's not *all* people but it is a likelihood and the more years we travel on this planet, the more likely it will happen, sometimes many times over. But as the old Chinese Proverb says, "Fall down seven times, stand up eight." Or maybe it's fall down 138 times, or 14,626…the point is, keep standing back up. The more times you get knocked down, the wiser you become. The wiser you become, the less likely it will happen again. Not by shutting off or hiding away, but by learning as well as becoming resilient.

People may say, "Well what if it was a murder or another horrific crime?" It is harder. It is not instant. It does take time and therapy or grief counseling can help a lot. But in those cases it's even more important to forgive *for yourself* so that you can actually have a life at some point. If it were a murder, that person who you love who is gone would not like to see you engulfed in anger towards their attacker for the rest of your life. No amount of anger or hatred would ever, ever bring them back. They would love to see you happy. They would love to see you honor their memory by remembering the great times you had with them and the love you shared. They would love to see you experience joy again.

Forgiving means not staying angry forever or holding a grudge about what has already happened. It doesn't mean trusting that they won't do the same thing again or that things will be the exact same as they were before. If a person is to stay in your life, even after forgiveness, changes, boundaries, and amends may have to take place before trust can be rebuilt. People may want to skip out on the consequence of having to work and be patient to rebuild trust, but that's not possible nor should you feel like you're an unforgiving person because you can't just pretend it's all fine. If someone deliberately drives your car into a lake, just because they say they are sorry and you forgive them, it doesn't mean the car is fixed nor that they are absolved of responsibility of fixing it just because you've forgiven them. Many people don't know this. They expect that a "sorry" and a show of remorse is their job done then try to blame you if you treat them differently or question things you didn't question before.

Rules of Forgiveness to Make it Work

I. *No cherry picking.*

> Throughout the whole experience, everything happened exactly the way it did. Looking back now, you may think, "oh I should have left there, or there, or there." But here's the thing, without necessarily giving them credit for anything, it will help a lot if you can pick out and feel gratitude for things within that time period. Like the dog you adopted or the child or children you had with them. Feeling that love and gratitude for these beings that had no other way of existing in your world besides the exact way everything happened will allow

you to forgive at least up until th
came into your existence.

2. ***The promises that weren't kept.***
    So they said they were going to go to some
    restaurant or on some trip or get you some
    gift and those things never happened.
    Awesome! They probably would have
    ruined the dinner or the trip had you gone,
    and if they did buy you that gift you may
    not want to even look at it now. So put
    those things in your own future. Give
    yourself the gift, go to that place for dinner
    or start saving up for that trip and go by
    yourself or with a friend who you know you
    will have a great time with. And if you did
    go to a place and they ruined it, go again
    and enjoy it. Make a new memory.

3. ***The time that was lost.***
    You can't get that back. You can't. No
    matter which way you turn it over in your
    mind or how much you regret it, it's gone.

Accept that fully. You're born anew each day. They already wasted enough of your life, the less you give to their memory now and in the future, the more you have left to enjoy. You will have processing and flashbacks but you will also need to start to train your mind to shift focus and be present in what's awesome now. Stop allowing their shadow presence to poison your current life. The more you do it, the easier it will be. The more you're able to be fully present, the less their memory will creep back in. They will become less and less significant and the pain will fade.

4.   **The lessons.**

You don't regret first and second grade as a waste of time, right? Like you don't think they should have just taught you 12th grade stuff when you were 6 years old else they were wasting your time. Learning comes at the pace it comes. What you were willing to put up with and create in your life was

what you thought was righ
it hadn't been them specifi
have been someone similar. T
were attracted to, not the .
turned down or didn't feel any connection
to. Any other type wasn't a possibility at
the time. But you did get to learn a lot
about self-worth, the need for boundaries,
what love is and isn't, and misplaced loyalty.
Those lessons are so very valuable in life.
They alone will prevent the same thing
from happening again. You've been
vaccinated for life as long as you put the
focus on yourself and really assess what
happened with the goal of healing and
ensuring you will be your own bff and
protector from here on out. Not in a
guarded way but in an immune way. You
know where certain paths lead now and you
can choose not to go down them again with
a different name and face beckoning you to
go there.

Meditation.

Before you go to sleep, take a bit of time to meditate using this Ho'oponopono inspired mantra set. Breathing deeply and focusing on the feeling of the cool air coming in, the warm air going out, relaxing your muscles section by section, imagine once you're relaxed being in a dark room and a door in front of you. Imagine that door opening and light behind it. Imagine that person behind the door, just standing there, not angry or happy or upset or anything. Just their presence, listening. Feel whatever you feel. The first few times, you'll probably feel anger or sadness or both. Then imagine yourself calmly saying to them:

I forgive you

I release you

Thank you

Goodbye

"I forgive you" remember, only means, "I'm taking my life back by releasing the resentment towards you for the past. I don't want to carry this around anymore."

"I release you," means you're not going to be a factor in my life anymore. I won't attach, compare, or bring your memory into my present life anymore. I will live my life in the present without your shadow hanging over it.

"Thank you." Thanks for nothing! No, thank you for these lessons. If I didn't learn them through you, I would have had to learn them through someone else *just like you.* That may have taken even longer and may have been even worse. So thank you for that dark chapter in my life that taught me how important it is to love myself.

Goodbye.

You can imagine yourself saying just the four phrases, taking as much time as you feel like in between each one. You can imagine letting your anger out on them about any or many past experiences. Just make sure to imagine them still standing there in the doorway blank faced. This is about you being heard and letting go of it all, not about imagining them to be any better than they were. If there's one thing you learned it's that you had to accept that's who they were and move on. Keep the focus on you and your feelings.

After the last "goodbye," imagine the door closing and take a deep breath. Let yourself feel again whatever emotions you're feeling. If you need to cry for another release, do it. If you feel relief, then awesome! And if you feel relief one day and cry the next, that's fine, too. Healing comes in waves. It's not linear. Some days are easier and some days are more difficult. You're moving in the right direction and you'll get through it.

Do it as often as you feel like. It could be every night, or if that's too much every week or so. Eventually you will get to a point where it doesn't bother you as much, not because it got any better but because you've processed it and decided to set it down so that you can get on with your new life. Your new, amazing life has no place for that junk anymore...just the wisdom of the lessons, leaving the pain behind as best you can.

To reiterate, after you forgive someone, you can still think they are a jerk if they are a jerk. Anger dissolves compassion and compassion dissolves anger. But even if you're not angry anymore, having been through the process of understanding why someone is the way they are, how something damaged them so that they lash out or don't trust or hide behind a wall of manipulation and lies…you can still think they're a jerk when they behave like one. Most everyone has been through some horrible stuff. That doesn't excuse treating people like nothing. Especially when you're an adult and you've been around the block a few times. If a pattern repeats then most likely it's not "everyone else" but it is the person who is the common denominator. Taking responsibility for one's actions is a choice. Even if a person was hurt deeply or abused as a child. That can't be changed and wasn't ever right, but as an adult, a person has the choice to work through those traumatic events and not hang on to that pain and allow it to harm anyone who crosses their path.

They don't need to know you have forgiven them and you don't need to try to be friends with them once you have. If you know you cannot trust them and are really done with that chapter of your life, you can forgive someone in your own heart and never see or speak to them again.

Holding on to resentment, or being unforgiving, actually keeps you tied to the energy that you don't want. That energy, if you believe in the law of attraction, will draw in more people, circumstances, and situations where you will feel it again in real time. This may explain having the exact same type of awful relationship over and over with different people. Unfortunately when this happens, a lot of people make sweeping stereotypes about *all women* or *all men*, not realizing it's not true at all. They don't stop to see that some of their friends and relatives have great relationships...or maybe they do see that but dismiss it as, "well you sure got lucky. All the rest are awful and the same." When you hold a belief, you're prone to a thing called cognitive dissonance, or in simple terms, you believe more of what you think is true and less of what you don't. So if one awful relationship made you wary of relationships in general and you're still angry with that person long after you've broken up, you'll carry that belief, that energy, and that story into your new relationships. You may be drawn to people who are similar in an attempt to win the battle this time. You

69

no attraction to people who don't fit that

d wonder why there's no "spark" even though they seem very nice. Anger resides in the arousal center of the brain...so when you feel anger you are excited/aroused and attracted to it. You may have even noticed that in a bad relationship as long as you were into the arguments, no matter how frustrating it got, you kept going back. It was only when the arguments lost their excitement or when you realized that it was a boring battle to keep reliving that you were finally able to separate from that person. If it doesn't make you angry, you won't be pulled towards it. Seems counter-productive, but from an evolutionary point of view, tying anger to attention makes sense. It triggers all the survival mechanisms, dopamine, adrenaline, the same rush as cocaine. In the wild, what would anger you? Likely an enemy or attack from a wild animal. In order to have the strength and attention to fight it off and survive, you'd have to have your attention on it until it was no longer a threat. We're not supposed to choose partners who cause chronic anger. Everyone gets mad at each other every once in awhile, but definitely if it's happening daily or many times a day, even though your survival anger attraction mechanism makes you want to keep going back, you'd be much better off stepping above your basest instincts and leaving that relationship.

6 LEVELS OF FORGIVENESS

There are different stages or levels of forgiveness, and not everyone will reach the last level towards everyone and everything. The thing is, it doesn't matter. As long as you get past level one, you are more free than you ever would be without it. And level one opens the door to level two, and so on.

Level Zero

The event, relationship, or circumstance is as alive today as it was when it happened. The retelling of the hurts is filled with passion – passionate anger, passionate sadness, or even passionate rage. No healing has taken place and the wound is kept fresh

---

every day. Every new day is ruined by the past. Over time, this pain may become so huge that a person turns to alcohol to numb it or to drugs to try to escape it. All new relationships are sucked in to the dark vortex of the past.

Level One

The event, relationship, or circumstance no longer is an everyday spoken presence. There's a relief that it's over. Non-threatening events or even phrases can trigger panicked flashback memories of the past but they don't happen as often over time. It no longer controls one's whole life. There's no desire to have that person make amends or fix what's been broken. To that extent, it has been accepted, though it still causes pain if it's triggered or spoken about.

Level Two

Lessons become visible. It's not much, but it is empowering because instead of being a victim of the past, you begin to sift through the experiences and discover what you have learned about yourself, your

74

worth, your resilience, that you will take with you into the future. You may still get triggered here and there but for the most part, you feel more grounded in your present day life. If someone asks about the past, you no longer have the passion in any retelling, although it is still painful. You are becoming more and more free of the old energy of powerlessness, constriction, and limitation.

Level Three

You feel you have officially accepted the past as the past and moved on. It no longer pops into your mind daily. When memories do come up, you don't feel hardly any reaction inside except a present moment gratitude that you're here now and free from that. Whether it's not relevant at all anymore and has no effect, or whether you've successfully adjusted to life; first by coping and then by building a new life, you've done it. You wouldn't go back and change things because it would mean giving up the life you've built since then.

Level Four

Complete forgiveness and gratitude for what happened. This level isn't possible for many cases, and it's not one that you should feel like you must strive for or have failed at forgiveness if you never reach it. Especially when lifelong injury or when the loss of life was part of it, it's just not a place your heart is willing to go. And that's totally ok. To be in this place requires an almost completely detached view of life and full acceptance that life's tragedies are a part of the story. It may not be reached during one's lifetime except right at the end, if time has been allowed to reflect on the whole and all grudges, resentments, anger, fear, or hatred wash away in the acceptance that life is about to be over and those things won't have any weight anymore.

The Path To Forgiveness

Forgiveness isn't linear. You don't hear a bell ring when you move up a level. You may feel you're at Level Three and all of a sudden a memory comes out of the blue and you're right back at Level Zero for a moment. Or an hour. Or a week.

The phrase "letting go" sounds like it should be instant and is as easy as letting loose the grasp of a balloon on a string but it's more like:

1. You become aware

2. You get fed up

3. You blow up

4. You blow up again while processing all the past stuff from your new perspective

5. You forgive

6. You move on, never to repeat the lesson again.

"Let it go" is a much overused phrase in inspiration but it has a lot of value in the right context. Once you've felt the anger, once you've learned the lesson, once you've processed the pain, you'll come to a point where you can choose to keep the pain alive and dwell on it or to set it down (i.e., let it go).

When this time is isn't up to anyone else but you. Other people may be sick of hearing about things that you're still processing and bark at you to "let it go already!" but that isn't in any way helpful or being a friend. It's not up to them to decide your healing for you. They wouldn't bark at someone recovering from an accident or an illness and emotional pain really isn't any different. It can be just as debilitating and can last longer than you ever wanted it to but that's how it is. If they can't seem to find compassion, don't talk to them about it anymore. But don't feel guilt or shame for not healing within a time frame that's convenient for them. Stay with you. Keep loving and encouraging yourself every day. Your strength and resilience, and ultimately your healing, will only come through that love and encouragement. Don't you ever give up on you.

Processing Time and Letting Go

When you get caught up in a damaging relationship, you usually lose focus of where you are, how low your standards keep dropping just trying to make things work and make the other person happy, and how you are feeling. After it's over, you will have several phases of healing. After the initial shock, there's a time period of grieving – both the future that isn't going to happen as you thought and the past that you'll start to see more clearly as you reflect. If someone dropped (or threw) a bowling ball on your foot and a minute later someone told you to let it go…you'd clearly be able to tell them that your foot is literally still in pain. A few days later, you could clearly point to a bruise. A few days after that, you could point out a bruise that's fading. When it comes to matters of the heart, it's the same but longer. The injury wasn't once and doesn't just go away in a few days even if you wanted it to. Healing will happen, but only with time and focused effort. It will happen in stages even with those. Physically, your body heals a basic wound on it's own. You do have to keep the wound clean, nourish your body with good foods, and allow time to pass. If it's a really bad wound you may need stitches or antibiotics or some other medical treatment. So for wounds of the heart…use the same method. Keep your heart as clean as you can. Don't suppress your anger or sadness or try to pretend it's not there when it is. But do treat yourself very well and choose to spend your time in positive ways, even if that means napping or having some solitary time – it is your healing. Some people may tell you to rush out and date a bunch of people after a breakup but that's rarely a good idea. It would only be a distraction and you may find it more difficult to process with so much "new other person energy" going on in your life. Nourish your mind with positive movies, TV shows, maybe even self-help or motivational videos and books to help sort out some of what you're feeling. Or just silly, fun stuff to get your mood up.

Forgiveness is resilience training.

It's not about "them" or thinking they're great in the end. Forgiveness doesn't mean you have to like them again…ever. It doesn't mean you hang out with them. It doesn't mean they've been absolved of the wrong that they did. Forgiveness means you no longer allow the weight of resentment towar

to control or govern your life in any way.

longer live in the past or allow it to poison your present views of yourself or other people. You no longer relive the pain as if it were happening real time. This is why forgiveness releases you from a prison. It allows you to live your life. Bad things happen to everyone. Horrible things happen to many people.

But once a horrible thing happens, it doesn't mean your life is over.

Resilience and the ability to set those horrible things down mentally and emotionally is the key to living a full and happy life. Recovering from especially horrible things may take time, effort, a variety of therapies to heal, but healing is possible. Even with scars. Healing is a choice and is possible. It is your gift to you and to all the wonderful people currently in your life and those who you haven't met yet. No one else will be punished or hurt by the pain from the past.

Why some things are harder to let go

Think about it physically. If someone accidentally barely bumped into you and immediately apologized, you wouldn't even be mad. You'd have instantly forgiven them.

But if someone who didn't like you for no reason came squealing around the corner in their car and drove straight into you on purpose and sent you to the emergency room, that wouldn't be so easy to forgive and healing would take some time and effort.

So there are a few things to consider:

1. If it was intentional or not

2. How much you were hurt

3. How long it went on

And one you may not have thought about,

4. How sensitive or unhealed you were about that previously.

Think again on the physical…if someone came up behind you and tapped your shoulder, that wouldn't hurt, right? But if you had a really bad sunburn and someone touched your back, even very lightly, even not realizing you had a sunburn…it would hurt and you would react.

So translating that into mental and emotional, or even physical too in cases of physical abuse, often times only you know what these things are, how much they hurt, how long it went on, and how healed you are at any given time. If someone doesn't know what you are going through, say in the case of a break up or divorce from a person who was abusive to you in one or all three ways. They may judge you or tell you that you should "just forgive" that person when they have absolutely no clue what they are talking about. In most abusive relationships, the abuse is hidden from the world so when the relationship ends, outside people have no idea what happened and thought you were such a great couple. And it's not their business. It's not their right to judge. You don't owe them any explanations. Just a firm, clear, defined boundary…for example, "I didn't ask for your advice, thank you. You don't know as much as you think you do, but I don't want to share with you."

The Forgiveness Difference

People who don't forgive say,
"I cannot accomplish something BECAUSE OF that person."
They feel that person or circumstance ruined them in some way and made them incapable of some good, desirable thing in life...a job, a loving relationship, happiness.

People who forgive say,
"I can accomplish something REGARDLESS of that person."
They feel that person or circumstance happened, but now it's over. Life can go on. They are still just as capable as they were before of good, desirable things in life. They do not let that person affect them anymore. They take control of their own life and their own happiness, and do not allow another person to rob them of great things that life has in store for them.

Remember, there are only two stories you can tell yourself about the person who wronged you; either they ruined your life forever or they were awful and now it's done and your life is wonderful because you've built it that way. Which story will you choose? If you've been certain of the first one for awhile, you've no doubt invited that shadow from your past into current situations. They've been an invisible unwanted guest at dinners with new people, their specter has been allowed to ruin events that reminded you of their presence, new, beautiful days that had nothing to do with them have been ruined because on the calendar they were markers for days from the past that were called anniversaries of the horrible.

7 BENEFITS OF FORGIVENESS

Holding on to the Anger is a Choice That Hurts You

You may think you have no choice. It happened and that's it. It's "unforgiveable" and now you're doomed so suffer the rest of your life. This just isn't true. For the most part, you are in control of your mind and where you put your thoughts. If you haven't trained your mind at all, it may be more difficult at first, but to become aware of your thoughts and consciously choose ones that are present day and positive, is to live empowered and free, more so every day.

Imagine forgiveness in the physical. Imagine if someone you knew one day threw a poisonous snake at you. The snake bit you and it hurt a lot. But then you held on to the snake. You were shocked and hurt and it was truly caused by that person. But now it's you holding the snake. When a new person comes by you say look at this snake, isn't it awful? And the snake is still terrifying and it keeps biting you but you continue to hold on to it because you think you have to. Nobody else can get near you because you are holding on to this angry snake so tightly and they could get bit, too, if they get too close. Maybe you think that as long as you hold on to it, you'll never forget that it's a possibility that someone can throw a snake at you. Well, pain makes a lousy shield. But if you decide to forgive, you put that snake down and let it go. Deciding to let go doesn't mean all of your wounds are healed instantly. But it does mean you won't relive the pain in real time over and over again and your wounds will begin to heal.

Forgiveness: What Benefits Are T˙ For You?

People say "forgiveness is for you, not them," and that is absolutely true, but if you hadn't realized that forgiveness is only about you and only about the past, you may not realize just how true it is.

When you forgive, when you set down the resentment and choose not to relive all those things that hurt you, you get your life back. You get your self back. You get to experience days and moments and times without the threat of the dark cloud of the past taking over at any time and ruining the new good moment. You become empowered to choose your life today and for your entire future. You don't subject anyone else to a lesser version of you who lashes out because they happen to use the same word or like the same pasta as someone who hurt you. You lose the over sensitivity to any past reminders and get to enjoy the world more. Roses can become roses again and not be awful reminders of tools of fake apologies that they once were.

Sundays can become Sundays again, not reminders of Sundays past that were committed to a certain pastime that a certain person from the past "made you" do. Tainted items, days, and experiences can regain their shine again and lost the pain that's been attached to them.

Once you relieve yourself of the outer anger or sadness directed towards "them," you can learn more about yourself. When you learn more about yourself and specifically your feeling and patterns, you can change the ones that cause pain.

Processing anger, hurt, sadness, or even being annoyed can teach you what your limiting beliefs are. From there, you can choose new beliefs and affirm them. Then, you will be more attracted to people and situations that support those beliefs and less attracted to those "lesson" ones that you won't need anymore.

If you say you are angry with "that person" for lying to you, what that means is you value trust. But if you choose to remain with a person who lies and try to change them to become a more truthful person, your belief may become that all people lie and hurt you. That belief will keep you attracted or tied to trying to change this person. If you truly believed that not all people lie or that your trust is valuable, you wouldn't be attracted to them. So work on your forgiveness of the past and on your beliefs for your present and future.

You may choose people who are condescending because you are not secure and confident in your worth. They will recreate situations where you will feel powerless and put down so that this belief comes true again and again. But when you foster your self-love, self-confidence, and self-worth, you won't feel a need to convince them or prove to them that you have those things. You will be sure of those qualities in yourself and won't be attracted to people who treat you the opposite of them.

So, what they did do for you was bring up "negative" emotions. Your negative emotions can teach you a lot about yourself. Avoiding them or trying to pretend they aren't there will often make them show up in more places and more often. Facing them and thinking about the belief that lies underneath them will allow you to decide to change that belief. That's when they will begin to dissolve.

As long as you are focused on that person or that ex or those people or your parents for being the way they were to you, you will remain stuck and will recreate those same situations with new names and faces. Forgiveness is freeing...literally. It frees you from the past pain and from recreating it with patterns and beliefs that you subconsciously choose over and over again. Your power is in your choices and beliefs. They don't create your life figuratively, they literally create your life – your surroundings, the people you choose to hold close, your view of yourself and the world around you. Your outer world is a mirror of your inner beliefs about yourself and about life.

Forgiveness: Revenge, Punishment, and Justice

Revenge: There is no winning in revenge. It just takes up more of a lifetime. Revenge is energy put towards destruction of another person, which could instead be put towards construction of the self. Revenge is trying to tear someone else's house down instead of rebuilding your own. It's giving even more time to a person who already took up enough time of your life. It's refusing to move forward and build a new life, but to try and keep destroying any remnant of the old life and prevent the other person from building anything in theirs. It may seem powerful but it isn't. It's stuck in the past. Your time here is limited. Use it wisely.

Punishment: When someone commits a crime, it seems fair that they will have some form of punishment. Punishment in the legal system involves returning a person to the state they would be if someone hadn't hurt, stolen, or broken something in their life. It's not retribution just for retribution sake, but a replenishment or return of things that were stolen.

Justice: Justice is important, not so much for the past, but for the present as a preventative for the future. Justice doesn't mean they got what they deserved, it means they won't be able to do the same to you or anyone else again in the future. If it was an actual crime and you go through the court system, it is important not to be consumed by and focus on that court process every moment of every day. If it consumes you entirely, it will be more pain than necessary. The intention of justice has to be of protection for self and for other innocent people who may be hurt in the future if the justice hadn't occurred. If it's not, then it will be an empty victory. It doesn't bring time back, and it won't bring a life back that was taken. It will keep you and other people safe in the future so that further pain won't be inflicted.

8 SHOULD THEY REMAIN IN YOUR LIFE?

This is a difficult decision, and one that comes to a conclusion with honest reflection and being aware of what you deserve and your boundaries. It also means not taking things personally.

Taking things personally seems to make sense; you're a person. But in our closest relationships, we are our most vulnerable. When vulnerability has been taken advantage of or is tied to pain, it's incredibly uncomfortable. So if a person were raised in a traumatic, violent, or abusive household, vulnerability by itself can become terrifying. If a 't aware of how their pain when not

ects onto everyone they love, they believe

and have defense mechanisms that will

override how they ideally would want to treat those who they love; partners or children. Taking their words and actions personally adds an extra layer of pain and with partners can blind you to what otherwise would be obvious. If you believe a partner has been abused, taken advantage of, or betrayed by their previous relationships and want to be *the one person* who shows them unconditional love and is trustworthy and supportive, those are all beautiful intentions. But if they view relationships as unsafe and vulnerability as weakness that leaves them open to being hurt, they will push you away via mistrust, unkind words, and at times even indifference. You may see them lying to other people but think they would never lie to you. They may have told you that you're the only one in the world they can trust and the one person in the world who isn't like the rest and that's a huge responsibility and pedestal. But then in the next breath, their defense mechanisms kick in and their words knock you off the pedestal they had built and it doesn't seem to make any sense. Maya Angelou famously said, "When a person shows you who they are, believe them the first time." This isn't a mean or unloving statement. It's a true statement. If you see people lie to others, you have to realize they lie and they will lie to you. If you see them cheat other people, or seek revenge, or insult or belittle, they will do those things to you. And you making them aware of any of this can seem helpful, but if they up to this point believe that's the best way for them to live their lives, especially in later adulthood, your well meaning and sincere words may be agreed with wholeheartedly on the surface but they will turn around later on and tell you that you're controlling and that nothing they do is good enough for you. Forgiving them does not mean to keep trying to have a close relationship with them. Forgiving them means to put yourself at a safe distance emotionally, mentally, and even physically so that they won't be able to harm you...even if that means not speaking at all. You can still love them from afar and have compassion for them inasmuch as you can see they are good underneath the pain they carry but that by holding onto their pain, they injure anyone who comes close. You can hope or pray that someday they see and take responsibility for their own healing, words, and actions. But change doesn't happen in an instant or with a revelation, and it doesn't happen with constant pressure to become better than they are. It comes from within and takes conscious effort and commitment and has to be for themselves and themselves only, not for you or just to keep you. It's not helping them to stay and it's not abandoning them to go. It may help them to see that if they continue they way they are, they will lose a good person and it will definitely protect your self-worth by not subjecting yourself to horrible treatment because you feel sorry for their inner child and can see things that they don't.

What if they apologize?

Was it a full and real apology?

A full and real apology contains five things:

1. A realization of what they did wrong

2. Taking responsibility for their words and actions

3. Expressing sincere remorse

4. An effort to make amends

5. Assurance that it won't happen again in the future.

The more you have of these, the less likely it is to happen again. The fewer you have of these, the more likely it will happen again. Especially if they don't even realize or pretend not to realize what they did wrong. Not taking responsibility means to dismiss, deny, diminish, or deflect. Dismiss is to say it was nothing or wasn't wrong at all. Deny is to try to put some lies on top. Diminish is to say it wasn't that bad or that hurtful or list good things they do which in no way has any relevance to what they have done. Deflect is to avoid all of the above and instead blame you for something or and to compare what friends do in their relationships to try to make you feel so lucky to have them.

When other people haven't forgiven people from their past, eventually they will speak to those people via projection while looking at you if you are in a close relationship or friendship with them.

Non-forgiveness is a dirty spot on the eyeglasses; no matter where you look, you see the spot. If a person doesn't realize the spot is on their own glasses, they will insist and totally believe that they see it on every person they look at. "All women are crazy" or "all men are liars" isn't true. It's a spot on the glasses.

When you meet someone, listen to them. If their past stories have them painted as the good guy or good woman and every relationship was with a user, liar, loser, or similar, listen to their reality. They believe that's who people are. They believe their role in life is to be the good one. So if you try and prove to them that you are a good one, too, eventually, they will project or make up things that make you the bad one…no matter how good you are or how much of yourself you lose in trying to be the best person they ever knew.

If a person has done their inner work; forgiven, accepted, come to terms with, realized their responsibility in choosing certain people and recreating painful dynamics, then the way they speak of their past won't sound the same way at all. It may sound like "I chose people who I thought I could save because I thought that was my job and it made me a good person." Or, "I felt insecure about my worth so I chose people who seemed to really need someone to fix and care for them but it was really me being controlling to placate my own insecurities and give me what I thought would be a secure role in their life and they wouldn't leave. But then I became their parent more than their partner and they rebelled against being controlled."

If someone sees themselves as a perpetual victim, you're going to be the next predator. Or they'll lose interest because you're not fulfilling the role in the dynamic and you won't know what you did wrong.

You've got to do your self-work and then seek to be close to people who have already done their self-work when you meet them. You can't turn into a guru and hand them your favorite books and try to fast track their growth. They have to realize and want to grow on their own…otherwise you'll later be told that nobody's perfect and look at all they've done for you and nothing's good enough for you. And those words will be a recreation of how they felt about their mother as a child and you'll have become their displeased mother who only had intentions of the best for them.

Well Meaning Versus Domineering Anchors

Well meaning anchors have a different view of you than you do. But it's not just you, it's life in general. They are very limited in what good they believe is actually possible for "people like us." If they say hurtful or discouraging things, it's 99% of the time coming from a place of worry and concern. They are not intentionally trying to discourage or hurt you, but it happens nonetheless. They are the accidental voice of doubt that you really don't need to hear when you're trying to level up. They can be the most kind and loving people. If you can let it bounce off you or steer the conversation away from their "helpful" advice and on to just about anything else, you won't find yourself leaping into the downward spiral of playing frustrated defense.

Conversely, **domineering anchors** are very insecure and need you to stay small for them to feel superior. They actually are trying to bring you down, discourage you, or hurt you. It makes them feel stronger than you and in control. If you did well in life or Heaven forbid better than them, it would strip them of their identity as the smartest person in the room. You may be able to keep them in your life without constantly getting hurt and forgiving yourself for putting yourself in that position again while knowing better, but you've really got to consider why you're doing that and if it's actually benefitting anyone.

9 REACHING OUT FOR CLOSURE

Should you contact someone after you've forgiven them, or after some time has passed to forgive them? For example, a person you used to have a romantic relationship with or an estranged family member, especially if you've heard they are ill and will pass away soon...

You've got to do what you feel is right. But the short answer is, maybe surprisingly, **no**.

In the movies they sometimes have scenes where someone is about to pass and they make a beautiful deathbed confession and have regret and offer a heartfelt apology to someone and that someone is so glad they met with them and now can feel closure and validation.

But listen.

If someone is ill and they actually feel that way and feel it's important enough to communicate it with you, they will reach out to you. In that case, it is true, you may regret not going to see them or at least talking to them and being part of them releasing an emotional burden. But that really would be for them.

Someone else's words and opinion can't bring you any more closure than what you could give to yourself.

You see, you have a story of what happened between you and to you, your story is true. The events that happened, the words that were said, and that you were hurt. But their story may be very different. They may have even rearranged or totally rewritten history to relieve themselves of guilt and made you out in their mind as the person who hurt or abandoned them and have forgotten all about the horrible or nasty things they said and ways they acted towards you. If that's the case, then the validation and release you may be trying to achieve with them could backfire into a shocking denial and defensive attack towards you.

So trying to have a hallmark moment may actually be more damaging in the end than just forgiving them in your heart and allowing your own closure to occur without confirmation from them. Remember, forgiveness is for you and only requires you to complete.

Conversely, if you were the one who was a jerk and want to reach out to someone to sincerely apologize, do it...with one exception. If it's an ex relationship and you seek them out on social media and see that they're married or in a relationship, it may be better to shelf that. If you truly care for them, you want to add, not subtract from their life, then to not contact them if they are married or in a relationship is doing so out of respect for their current life and their current relationship. Your apology ultimately is about relieving your own conscience and making amends in your own mind and heart. The last thing you'd want to do is inadvertently stir up some drama up in their life.

Other than that...do it. Even if they never reply, even if they don't accept your apology, do it. That will be for your conscience and to make sure you have taken responsibility for your words and actions which can help provide closure for you in your forgiveness to yourself.

It may be received well by them, it may help them, it may not affect them at all...those reactions are totally out of your control and you can't predict what they will be. You can only control your actions and the energy you choose to extend to someone else. By extending a sincere apology, you are extending the energy of appreciation and love to them, and regardless of if you even speak again after that, it will be an experience of maturing for you.

Accepting responsibility, having the courage to be vulnerable and display your past flaws...that's maturity.

That is true change and growth.

10 DAILY FORGIVENESS

There are plenty of opportunities every day to get mad or feel hurt. For the most part, many people feel it's just part of life and that's how people are. But every little resentment is a little dent in your wellbeing. Whether you had a rude cashier or were cut off in traffic, how you choose to process those events will shape in tiny ways your view about people and the world. Forgive little things and negative encounters with strangers instantly and consciously. Even if you make up a story to go with it. The person who was rude could be having a horrible day. The person who cut you off in traffic could just be an awful driver. That's just what they're going through or who they are right now. If you got what you needed at the store and were able to still be kind to the rude person, you got what you needed and maybe left them with something they needed. If you were cut off in traffic but didn't get into an accident, well that was some luck shining down on you and hopefully that person will learn to drive more carefully for their own sake and for others. You can consciously let these things roll off you like water off a duck's back or you can subconsciously or consciously allow them to seep in and add up. If you allow them to seep in, they can sour your overall mood. If you bring attention to how awful they are each time you'll end up convinced that ALL cashiers are rude or ALL drivers in your *entire state* are awful drivers. That will end up creating an energy in you that will ensure you'll more often than not have more negative experiences. Belief drives reality. If you eventually believe something, you bring in the attitude that it's true and end up creating it in reaction rather than action. So it will stay true for you.

Consciously choose to forgive instantly or if you felt like you were in danger like in the car cutting you off in traffic, let the fear, shock, and anger pass through you and then insert those grateful statements like, "thank goodness I avoided an accident" or "I must have someone watching over me to have stayed safe." We believe what we tell ourselves. Why not tell yourself a positive story instead of a negative one? What happened and where you are will be the same, it's only the story that's attached that will leave you in a foul or good mood.

And before bed, if you're working through a deeper emotional injury, do that forgiveness meditation each night and allow your inner psyche to chip away and release those old hurts little by little. As you release them, you change your beliefs. And especially with the parental hurts, those beliefs didn't end when you turned 18, any that were left can keep being recreated throughout an entire lifetime if they're not cleared by forgiveness. You may even find that you go through the meditation forgiving one person but as you do, memories of childhood and the real root of that pain comes to your consciousness. As you clear it, you won't subconsciously project or seek out people to recreate those old dynamics anymore. They are familiar – literally meaning from the family – but they are not comfortable, not beneficial, and you'll be a lot happier without them...as will the people who currently surround you and who will in the future.

Without forgiveness, you can't have full, open, complete gratitude. There will be parts of your heart still locked up with resentment. Without full gratitude, you are constricted from enjoying life to the fullest. If you were outright robbed of time or of good parts of yourself at some point in your life, the best thing you can do for yourself is free up your heart and enjoy the time you still have here, now, and in the future.

ABOUT THE AUTHOR

Doe Zantamata was born and raised in Canada near Toronto. She attended university at Niagara University for two years before transferring to Florida State University and holds a BSc. in Biology. From there, she pursued many creative projects, including independent films, acting, and graphic design. She has been writing since the time she could hold a pen, but launched her social media pages in April 2011. The book series, "Happiness in Your Life," is a set of twelve short books, each on a specific aspect of life but all intertwined together in many ways.

Please visit:

www.HappinessInYourLife.com

and the blog:
www.theHiYL.com

Printed in Great Britain
by Amazon